The Six Wives of Henry VIII

by Catherine Allison

Contents

Longman

Edinburgh Gate
Harlow, Essex

Introduction

When Henry VIII became King of England in 1509, he was young, handsome and well-educated. He was also looking for a wife. But he could not marry a woman just because he loved her. He wanted to make sure that his family kept the crown of England after his death. To do this, he needed a wife who could give him male children. The woman he married could also make a difference to how England got on with other countries – whether there was peace or war – so Henry had to choose carefully.

Henry VIII was unusual because he married six times in trying to have sons and keep the kingdom at peace. Each time he married, he thought that he had found the perfect wife. But each wife disappointed him in some way … and he could be cruel when he was disappointed. By the end of his life, Henry had divorced two wives, he had two more executed, and he had only three living children.

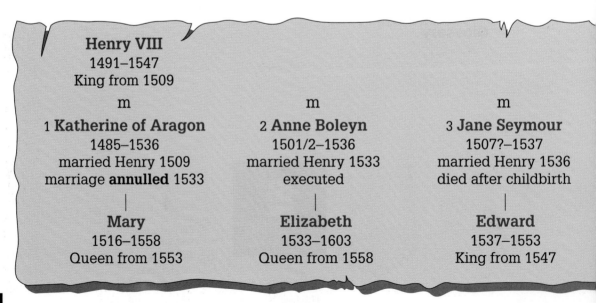

Henry VIII
1491–1547
King from 1509

m

1 **Katherine of Aragon**
1485–1536
married Henry 1509
marriage **annulled** 1533

Mary
1516–1558
Queen from 1553

m

2 **Anne Boleyn**
1501/2–1536
married Henry 1533
executed

Elizabeth
1533–1603
Queen from 1558

m

3 **Jane Seymour**
1507?–1537
married Henry 1536
died after childbirth

Edward
1537–1553
King from 1547

King Henry VIII in 1509, when he was 18

m	m	m
4 **Anne of Cleves**	5 **Katherine Howard**	6 **Katherine Parr**
1515–1557	1521?–1542	1512–1548
married Henry 1540	married Henry 1540	married Henry 1543
marriage annulled 1540	executed	

Katherine of Aragon

(1485–1536)

Katherine was the daughter of the King and Queen of Spain. At this time, Spain was one of the most powerful countries in the world. When she was 15, Katherine married Prince Arthur, who was Henry's elder brother. He died only five months later. For a long time, Katherine did not know what would happen to her. Then, when Henry became King seven years later, he married her. Katherine was his first wife.

Katherine was beautiful. She had long, wavy, golden hair and large blue eyes. She was a clever woman and also very religious. She always did what her new husband told her to do. Henry was fond of her, and the English people loved her too.

At first the two of them were very happy, but Katherine could not give Henry a son. She had six children but only one daughter, Mary, lived. Henry began to think that God was punishing him for marrying his dead brother's wife, and that was why they could not have a son.

Katherine of Aragon, aged 16

By the time she was 40, Katherine was probably too old to have any more children. Then Henry fell in love with one of her **maids of honour**, Anne Boleyn. He began to look for a way to end his marriage to Katherine.

Henry wanted his marriage to Katherine **annulled**. That would mean that the marriage had never been legal and that Katherine had never been Queen. It would also mean that their daughter Mary was **illegitimate**. England was a Catholic country, so the **Pope** was the only person who could annul the marriage – but he would not do it. So Henry ignored the Pope, and had the marriage ended by his own religious men. This was the first step to England becoming a Protestant country.

Katherine pleaded with Henry to change his mind and keep their marriage alive.

Katherine fought Henry over this, but in the end Henry sent her away from the royal court. She never stopped loving Henry – even when he married Anne Boleyn and made her his queen. She signed herself "Katherine the Queen" until the day she died.

Anne Boleyn

(1501 or 1502–1536)

Anne Boleyn was charming, witty and very clever. She spent some years as maid of honour to the French Queen and then came to Henry's court. She was 20 years old and she was the most fashionable lady there. She was very popular with the young men at court, and the King fell in love with her.

Henry wanted Anne to be his **mistress**, but Anne refused. She said he had to make her his wife and Queen of England. She was determined to have her own way and not give in. She made him wait for six years.

The badge of Anne Boleyn:
a crowned falcon and the Tudor rose

Anne Boleyn, painted when she was Queen

Henry could not marry Anne until his marriage to Katherine of Aragon was annulled. But in the end he could wait no longer. He married Anne in secret, four months before the annulment of his marriage to Katherine of Aragon.

Anne was crowned Queen in London on 1st June 1533.
She used some of her wealth and power to help people
who were against the Roman Catholic Church. This made
people think that she was a bad influence on Henry. Some
even thought that she was a witch. They said she had six
fingers on one hand.

Anne gave birth to a daughter, Elizabeth, whom she loved
very much. But Henry still longed for a boy. Anne was
pregnant three more times, but none of the babies lived.
Henry was very disappointed. He felt that Anne had
betrayed him.

In 1535, Henry fell in love with one of Anne's maids of honour. Her name was Jane Seymour and Henry wanted to marry her. His men set out to prove that Anne was guilty of **adultery**, and of plotting to murder him. The punishment for this was death. Anne had always been popular with the young men at court, so people found it easy to believe that she was guilty of adultery.

We don't know if Henry really believed that she was guilty or if he just wanted her out of the way. It made no difference. Anne was arrested for **treason**. She was found guilty and sentenced to death. She was beheaded at the Tower of London on 19th May 1536. Henry had his marriage to her annulled, and he never mentioned her name again.

Jane Seymour

(1507?–1537)

Jane Seymour was a **maid of honour** to Katherine of Aragon, Henry's first wife, and then to his second wife, Anne Boleyn. Henry may have first fallen in love with Jane in the autumn of 1535 when he and Anne visited her family home in Wiltshire. She seemed quiet and obedient, which was just what Henry wanted in a wife.

Jane was not as well educated as Katherine or Anne had been, but she was still determined to become Queen. Henry gave her gifts but she kept him at a distance. She was determined to be his wife, not his **mistress**. He once gave her a purse of gold coins, but she returned the gift unopened saying that she would not let him treat her like a mistress. After that, Henry agreed to see her only when her family were with her. In that way there would be no gossip about their relationship before they were married. The wedding took place on 30th May 1536, less than two weeks after Anne Boleyn's execution.

The badge of Jane Seymour: a phoenix, castle and Tudor roses

Jane Seymour, painted in 1537

Jane was a Roman Catholic so she wanted Henry to make peace with the **Pope**. She was also sympathetic to Catholic people in England who protested when Henry closed religious houses, such as **abbeys**, to take their money and land. When she pleaded with him not to close the abbeys, he became very angry. He told her that the last Queen had died because she argued with him too much. Jane was terrified that Henry would get rid of her too, so she decided never to discuss such things with Henry again.

However, there was one other thing Jane wanted Henry to do. Henry was unkind to his daughter Mary because she had taken her mother's side when their marriage was **annulled**. Jane wanted Henry to forgive Mary, but she knew that this subject could make him angry. She had learnt her lesson about arguing with Henry. She was very careful when she spoke to him about it and always waited until he was in a good mood. Eventually Henry forgave his daughter and he and Mary were **reconciled**.

Mary, daughter of Henry VIII and Katherine of Aragon

Henry VIII with Edward and Jane Seymour by his side

In January 1537, Jane became pregnant. Henry was delighted, and ordered all the church bells in London to ring in celebration. Jane gave birth to a healthy son, Edward, on Friday 12th October, but she soon fell seriously ill. Twelve days later, with Henry at her bedside, Queen Jane died.

Henry said that Jane was his most beloved wife. He **commissioned** this painting years after her death in 1543, which shows Jane at the centre of the Tudor family. Henry was buried in the same tomb with her when he died.

Anne of Cleves

(1515–1557)

Henry's fourth wife was Anne of Cleves, a German princess. Henry wanted another son in case his baby son Edward died before he could inherit the crown. His advisers chose Anne because Germany was a Protestant country. They thought that his marriage to her would bring the two countries together. Germany would be an **ally** and help England stand up to any Catholic enemies in Europe.

The couple did not meet until just before their wedding. Henry had seen a portrait of Anne that showed her to be beautiful, but when he finally met her, he thought she was ugly. He said he could not love her.

The badge of Anne of Cleves

Anne of Cleves – the portrait shown to Henry VIII before he married her

The couple were married on 6th January 1540, but Henry was determined that they would not stay married long. Anne tried hard to please Henry, but she had very little in common with him. She could not speak English and did not dance or play any musical instruments, while Henry loved to do these things. He was so polite to her in public, however, that it was some weeks before Anne realised that he didn't like her.

By April, Henry was falling in love with Katherine Howard, one of Anne's maids of honour. Anne never disliked Katherine because of this, but she was afraid that Henry would treat her badly if he wanted to marry Katherine.

Hever Castle in Kent. This was the childhood home of Anne Boleyn. Henry gave it to Anne of Cleves.

Henry expected Anne to fight and argue when the marriage was declared over. To his surprise, she quietly accepted the decision – she was simply glad that nothing worse was going to happen to her. Henry gave her money, land and several grand houses to live in, and the freedom to marry again.

Anne became a rich, independent woman. She remained friends with Henry for the rest of his life, and his children often visited her. She never married again, but lived quietly in the country; she was respected by the King's family and was popular with the people of England. Anne outlived Henry and died just a few weeks before her 42nd birthday. Henry's daughter Mary, the Queen, arranged for her to be buried as a princess would be, in Westminster Abbey.

Katherine Howard

(1521?–1542)

Katherine Howard married Henry on 28th July 1540, when she was about 19 years old. She was a nobleman's daughter, and cousin to Anne Boleyn, Henry's second wife. Both her parents had died, but she had numerous brothers and sisters, and lived in the large household of her grandfather's wife. Her uncle, the Duke of Norfolk, wanted her to become Queen in order to increase his own power and ability to influence the King.

Henry was passionately in love with her. He believed that at last he had found the perfect wife. Katherine was a pretty teenager who loved dancing and fine clothes but, unfortunately, she did not know how a queen should behave.

Katherine was not as innocent as Henry believed her to be, and in 1541 details of her earlier life started to come to light. With no mother to look after her, she had been allowed to run wild. She had fallen in love at 17 with a young man who lived in her grandmother's household, and had agreed to marry him.

Henry was shocked when he heard all this, but he still loved her. He asked for more investigations to be made, hoping that they would prove her innocent of any worse crime. However, when she had become Queen, Katherine had given her childhood sweetheart a job at court. This made it look as if their relationship was still continuing behind Henry's back. Then a recent letter to another lover was found in Katherine's rooms. That was evidence of adultery, and Katherine's fate was sealed. Henry broke down in tears when he heard about the letter. He believed that she had betrayed him.

Katherine Howard

25

While Henry's advisers were collecting evidence against her, Katherine was confined to her rooms at Hampton Court Palace. She tried to see Henry once when he visited the palace, but the guards dragged her away screaming. That convinced her that she would die for her foolishness.

It was said that she was practising dance steps with her ladies in waiting when the King's guards came to arrest her. They took her to the Tower of London, where she was questioned until she confessed. When she was told that she was going to die, she asked that her family should not be harmed because of her – even though they had deserted her to save themselves. She also asked if she could practise putting her head on the executioner's block so that she would appear calm and brave when her last moment came. The men accused of being her lovers were arrested, tortured and executed.

Katherine was beheaded on 13th February 1542. She was only about 20 years old, and she was the last woman whom Henry would passionately love.

Katherine Parr

(1512–1548)

Katherine Parr was Henry VIII's last wife. She had been married twice by the time she met Henry, once when she was 17, and again when she was 21. Her second husband was dying, but Henry thought her attractive and decided to marry her as soon as she became a widow.

When the time came, however, Katherine did not want to marry Henry. She was in love with a handsome young **courtier**, Thomas Seymour, brother of the late Queen Jane. But Henry was determined to marry her, and sent Seymour abroad to get him out of the way. Katherine could not refuse a proposal of marriage from the King, so she decided to put all thoughts of Thomas out of her mind, and married Henry on 12th July 1543.

Thomas Seymour

Katherine Parr

By now, Henry was 52; he was very fat, balding, and with one leg so swollen that he was often unable to walk. Katherine was only 30, but she was the perfect wife for his old age. Her second husband had been much older than her, and she had been a loving stepmother – just as she would be for Henry's children. Of all his wives, she was Henry's best **companion**.

Katherine was very intelligent and well-educated; under her influence, the court became a centre for **scholarship** and women's education. She loved to argue about religion with her husband and published several books of her views, which was very unusual for a woman at that time. She encouraged Henry's Church reform, and is believed to have secretly been a Protestant – which was illegal during Henry's reign. She was nearly arrested for her views in 1546, but discovered that she was in danger just in time. She rushed to see the King and convinced him that she was innocent. After that, she didn't argue with Henry about religion any more.

As well as being clever, Katherine was always a kind stepmother to Henry's children. She encouraged her stepdaughters Mary (now in her twenties) and Elizabeth to write about religion as she had done. She helped to provide a more stable family home for them, and organised the education of Elizabeth and Edward. She grew very fond of Henry, and nursed him as he got older and became more and more ill.

When Henry died on 28th January 1547, Katherine left the court. She was now free to marry whoever she wanted, and she chose Thomas Seymour who had recently returned from abroad. The couple married in secret in the spring of that year.

Katherine had always wanted a child, and was delighted to discover that she was pregnant in March 1548. Sadly, immediately after the birth of her daughter in August, Katherine became dangerously ill, and died early in September. She was buried in the chapel of her husband's home, Sudeley Castle, Gloucestershire.

Glossary

abbey a place where monks or nuns live and worship

adultery a sexual relationship between a married person and someone who is not their wife or husband

ally a country that works closely with another country

annulled cancellation of a marriage, similar to divorce

commissioned instructed an artist to paint a picture

companion a friend who lives with another person and looks after them

courtier a nobleman who attended the King at his court

illegitimate a child whose parents are not married

maids of honour unmarried noblewomen who attended the Queen

mistress a woman who has a relationship with a married man

Pope the leader of the Roman Catholic Church, who lives in Rome

reconciled on good terms again after an argument

scholarship great learning

treason a crime against a person's country, King or Queen